Ohio
Plants and Animals

Marcia Schonberg

Heinemann Library
Chicago, Illinois

© 2003 Heinemann Library
a division of Reed Elsevier Inc.
Chicago, Illinois

Customer Service 888-454-2279

Visit our website at www.heinemannlibrary.com

Designed by Heinemann Library
Photo research by Beth Chisholm
Printed and bound by Lake Book Manufacturing

07 06 05 04 03
10 9 8 7 6 5 4 3 2 1

Library of Congress Cataloging-in-Publication Data
Schonberg, Marcia.
   Ohio plants and animals / Marcia Schonberg.
      p. cm. -- (Heinemann state studies)
Summary: Describes the plant and animal communities which live in
Ohio's
various ecosystems, including woodlands, streams and lakes, wetlands,
and
urban areas.
Includes bibliographical references (p.   ).
   ISBN 1-4034-0669-3 (hc) -- ISBN 1-4034-2691-0 (pb)
   1. Animal communities--Ohio--Juvenile literature. 2. Plant
communities--Ohio--Juvenile literature. 3. Zoology--Ohio--Juvenile
literature. 4. Botany--Ohio--Juvenile literature. [1. Zoology--Ohio.
2.
Botany--Ohio.] I. Title. II. Series.
   QH105.O3S36 2003
   578'.09771--dc21

2002154206

Acknowledgments
The author and publishers are grateful to the following for permission to reproduce copyright material: title page (L-R) David Hosking/Photo Researchers, Inc., Hal Horwitz/Corbis, Gary Micaron/Visuals Unllmited; contents page (L-R) A. Rider/Photo Researchers, Inc., Scott T. Smith/Corbis, Mark & Sue Werner/The Image Finders; p. 4 David Muench/Corbis; p. 5 Maslowski/Visuals Unlimited; pp. 6, 37, 45 maps.com/Heinemann Library; pp. 7, 28T D. Robert & Lorri Franz/Corbis; pp. 8, 23B Carl A. Stimac/The Image Finders; p. 10T Scott T. Smith/Corbis; pp. 10B, 16T, 39 Hal Horwitz/Corbis; p. 11T Tom Uhlman/Visuals Unlimited; p. 11B Scott Camazine/Photo Researchers, Inc.; pp. 12, 25T, 35 Mark & Sue Werner/The Image Finders; pp. 13, 17B Dan Tyrpak/The Image Finders; p. 15 William J. Weber/Visuals Unlimited; p. 16B Kennan Ward/Corbis; p. 17T Tom Brakefield/Corbis; p. 18T Steve Austin/Papilio/Corbis; p. 18B Gary Micaron/Visuals Unlimited; p. 19 Larry Miller/Photo Researchers, Inc.; p. 20 Gary Meszaros/Visuals Unlimited; p. 21 Pat Anderson/Visuals Unlimited; p. 22 Nick Bergkessel/Photo Researchers, Inc.; p. 23T Ron Austing/Photo Researchers, Inc.; pp. 24, 28B, 30 Joe McDonald/Corbis; p. 25B Peter Reynolds/Frank Lane Picture Agency/Corbis; pp. 26, 34 Jim Baron/The Image Finders; p. 27T Richard Hamilton Smith/Corbis; p. 27B A. Rider/Photo Researchers, Inc.; p. 29T Gary Meszaros/Photo Researchers, Inc.; p. 29B Eric and David Hosking/Corbis; p. 31 Jim Baron/The Image Finders; pp. 32, 38B Mary Ann McDonald/Corbis; p. 33T William A. Bake/Corbis; p. 33B Ken Brate/Photo Researchers, Inc.; p. 36 Ohio Department of Natural Resources; p. 38T Gerard Fuehrer/Visuals Unlimited; p. 40 David Hosking/Photo Researchers, Inc.; p. 41 The Cleveland Museum of Natural History; p. 42T James L. Amos/Corbis; p. 42B Tom McHugh/Photo Researchers, Inc.; p. 43 Rick and Nora Bowers/Visuals Unlimited; p. 44 Bettmann/Corbis

Cover photographs by (top, L-R) Pat Anderson/Visuals Unlimited, Gary Micaron/Visuals Unlimited, Ohio Department of Natural Resources, Dan Tyrpak/The Image Finders; (main) Mark & Sue Werner/The Image Finders

Every effort has been made to contact copyright holders of any material reproduced in this book. Any omissions will be rectified in subsequent printings if notice is given to the publisher.

Some words are shown in bold, **like this.** You can find out what they mean by looking in the glossary.

Contents

Introduction

Ohio's earliest peoples thrived in the thick forests and clear streams that they found in the area. Native Americans discovered woods and rivers alive with many **resources** for hunting, gathering, and trading.

Early explorers told stories about the land. They said that the land was so thick with forests, squirrels could jump from branch to branch and never have to come down from the trees. The rivers were so full of fish that they could be scooped out with bare hands. The ground was so fertile, crops grew easily. Today, these stories may sound like tall tales. Yet they attracted early settlers with a sense of adventure to head west-

Today, many Ohio forests are state parks. Conkles Hollow, shown here, is a state nature preserve.

ward toward Ohio. They wanted to see for themselves the land between Lake Erie and the Ohio River.

In the 1700s, European settlers started to arrive in the area that is now Ohio. They spread the word about the **fertile** land back to the colonies on the Atlantic coast. When the colonists heard about the area's richness, many became eager to travel there. By the early 1800s, many Europeans had settled in the area that is now Ohio.

Early settlers hunted raccoons for food and for their furs.

To an early settler, Ohio's resources may have seemed limitless. But today, the wildlife, trees, and other plants are not as plentiful as the early explorers and settlers described. Ohio has changed greatly since the Native Americans and European explorers traveled the Great Lakes, the Ohio River, and the many inland streams in the state.

As Ohio grew into an industrial and populated state, much of its natural resources and open spaces were used. Settlers cut down many trees in order to settle on the land. So, forests decreased and vanished in many parts of Ohio. **Prairies** disappeared as more farms were settled. As a result, natural **habitats** for the wildlife that lived in these areas also decreased or vanished. Today, forests, **streams, wetlands,** and **urban** areas in Ohio are still home to many kinds of plants and animals. However, some of the species that once thrived there have become **extinct, endangered,** or **extirpated.**

Ohio Ecosystems

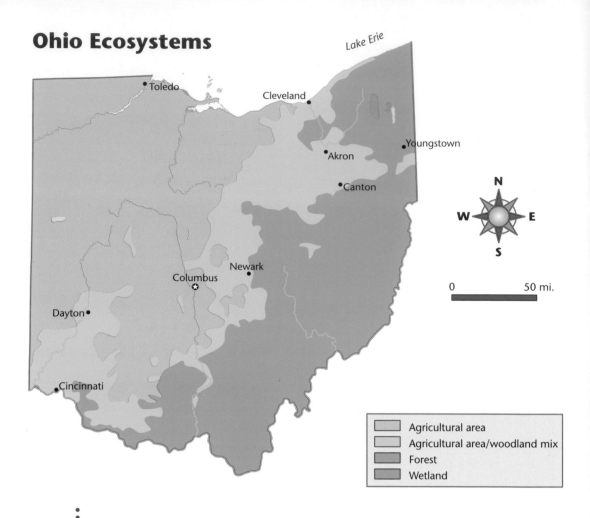

Lake Erie

Toledo
Cleveland
Akron
Youngstown
Canton
Newark
Columbus
Dayton
Cincinnati

0   50 mi.

Agricultural area
Agricultural area/woodland mix
Forest
Wetland

Today, Ohio's natural ecosystems overlap with agricultural developments.

Although Ohio's land and other resources have decreased because of settlement, Ohioans have worked hard to rebuild local **ecosystems.** Many people living in Ohio today work to promote ecology. This is the way that plants, animals, and humans live in the **environment.**

Ohio has set up many environmental programs. The Ohio **legislature** has passed laws to protect the state's resources and environment. These programs and laws have helped Ohio grow and restore the natural areas that once covered the state.

Endangered, Extinct, and Extirpated

The three "Es" are an important part of Ohio's natural history.

1. *Endangered* means that there are very few members of a plant or animal species remaining in an ecosystem. These species are protected by **conservation** groups, which try to prevent the endangered species from leaving their habitat. The peregrine falcon is an endangered animal in Ohio.

2. *Extinct* wildlife, plants, and animals are those that once lived in an ecosystem but no longer live there or anywhere else. The passenger pigeon is an extinct animal in Ohio and everywhere else.

3. *Extirpated* describes a species that once lived in an ecosystem but has now disappeared. These animals or plants may continue to live in other places, however, so they are not extinct. Elk and timber wolves (left) are examples of extirpated animals in Ohio. As settlers cleared Ohio's woods to make way for farmland and towns, these and other animals fled to nearby states. Extirpated species can return. In Ohio, this happened with the white-tailed deer. This species of deer disappeared in the early 1900s because its **habitat** was destroyed and it was overhunted. But the deer returned as forests were replanted and hunting laws were passed. In fact, this once extirpated animal is now Ohio's state mammal. Today, white-tailed deer are a very common sight throughout Ohio's woodlands.

Forests

A forest is home to many different plants and animals. Much of the forests, or woodlands, in Ohio are new. The forests there today are not the exact same forests the Native Americans and early Europeans found when they arrived. Nine out of every ten of Ohio's original forests were cut down to create farmland and to build settlements. Most of Ohio's new forests have been planted in the last 100 years.

Most of Ohio's woodlands were cleared before the government began protecting these natural **habitats.** When forests are cleared, many changes occur. The plants and animals that live there cannot survive. However, **conservation** programs today are helping forests grow again.

The leaves of deciduous trees turn bright colors before they fall.

The Ohio Department of Natural Resources protects and maintains natural areas in Ohio. The Ohio Division of Forestry supports two **nurseries** that grow between five and seven million tree **seedlings** each year. Ohioans then purchase these seedlings and plant them around the state. Each year, Ohioans plant more than fifteen million trees. Because of efforts such as these, today about eight million acres of land—about one third of the state—are covered by forests.

PLANT LIFE IN THE FORESTS

There are forests in every county in Ohio, but Southeastern Ohio is the most heavily wooded. About 97 percent of Ohio's forests is made up of **deciduous** trees. These kinds of trees lose their leaves at a certain time each year, then later grow new leaves. Before the leaves fall, they turn bright shades of gold, red, or orange during the warm days and cool evenings of fall. There are more than 100 different kinds of deciduous trees in Ohio.

Deciduous Trees

- ash
- aspen
- American beech
- birch
- boxelder
- buckeye
- eastern cottonwood
- elm
- maple
- oak

An Ancient Forest

There is a place in Ohio where you can see ancient oak trees like the ones that were around before the Native Americans or early settlers came to Ohio. Ancient oaks still grow in Dysart Woods, a 50-acre woods owned by Ohio University. Dysart Woods is located near Athens, in southeastern Ohio. It is one of Ohio's few remaining original forests. There, a 300-year-old oak tree can be more than 140 feet tall and 4 feet across.

The Importance of Trees

The Ohio Division of Forestry has a long list of reasons why trees are important. Here are just ten reasons to plant trees:

1. To provide shade
2. To produce oxygen for animals to breathe
3. To produce food
4. To provide a habitat for animals
5. To provide energy
6. To provide wood for construction
7. To reduce **erosion**
8. To give us Christmas trees that can be replanted
9. To produce pulp fiber to make paper
10. To make our cities and homes beautiful

The other three percent of Ohio's forests are **coniferous** trees. Coniferous trees stay green throughout the year. They have needle-shaped leaves. They grow new leaves before shedding the old ones. **Coniferous** trees have cones that hold the seeds for new trees.

Wildflowers, shrubs, and plants add to the variety of Ohio's forests. White trillium, Ohio's official wildflower, blooms in early spring. The trillium gets its name from the Latin word for *three*. The trillium has three

Two wildflowers found in Ohio's forests are pictured to the left: white trillium (top) and pink lady's slipper (bottom).

Hueston Woods State Park

Hueston Woods State Park, in southwestern Ohio, is part of the Till Plain region, where rich soil makes good farmland.

Most of the original trees in this area were cleared to make space for farming. But one 200-acre grove of ancient beech and sugar maple trees has been protected and exists today. The forest is a National Natural Landmark. In this forest you will also find many wildflowers, even rare ones such as the jack-in-the-pulpit (above, left). More than one hundred different kinds of birds and many animals, including Ohio's state snake, the Black Racer (left), also live in these woods.

flower petals and three leaves. Other wildflowers include the toothwort, the yellow-trout lily, and the pink lady's slipper orchid. Ohio's forests also include morel mushrooms, which can be found in April and May.

ANIMALS IN THE FORESTS

Many of the animals in Ohio's forests stay through all four seasons. Footprints of the white-tailed deer cross muddy or snow-covered paths, depending on the time of year, in every Ohio county. White-tailed deer have always been important animals in Ohio. They have been in Ohio since the Ice Age. They were important to many of Ohio's **prehistoric cultures.** Before European settlers came to Ohio, the white-tailed deer was the major food source for Ohio's Native Americans. European settlers hunted the deer for their skins. As more settlers came to Ohio, the number of deer decreased. By the beginning of the 1900s, white-tailed deer were **extirpated** from Ohio. But in the 1930s and 1940s, Ohio started **restocking** the deer. Many deer also began **migrating** back to Ohio from other states. By the mid–1990s, more than half a million white-tailed deer lived in Ohio.

Other animals also make Ohio's forests their home. The gray squirrel lives throughout the state and, like the white-tailed deer, stays in Ohio for the cold winter. Wild turkeys are rarely seen, but can be heard around the state. These wild turkeys were plentiful in the days of early settlers, but had disappeared by 1904. Today, about 250,000 of these once-extirpated animals now live in the wild in Ohio.

Ohio's State Animal

In 1986, fourth graders at Worthington Estates Elementary School, near Columbus, studied Ohio's state symbols. They decided Ohio needed an official state animal. The students learned how important the white-tailed

deer, pictured at left, was to the survival of early Ohioans. They wrote letters explaining this and other facts about the deer to state **legislators.** They presented their letters personally during several field trips. The state legislators liked their ideas and wrote a **bill.** Two years later, on February 10, 1988, students watched as Ohio legislators voted to make the white-tailed deer Ohio's official state mammal.

Several species of birds live in Ohio. The gray catbird lives in the **brush** areas on the edges of Ohio's forests. The

Wild turkeys can weigh up to 24 pounds.

catbird is known for imitating the sounds that it hears around it. This songbird **migrates** to Ohio in the spring and then it leaves in early fall. The brown thrasher also makes its home in the brush areas of Ohio's forests.

The five-lined skink is a reptile that makes its home in Ohio's forests. It gets its name from the five stripes on its body. Skinks are one of the fastest reptiles in the world. If a **predator** captures the skink by the tail, the tail breaks off, giving the skink time to escape. The tail grows back, but not to the same length.

The black racer is also a fast reptile. This snake lives on the floor of Ohio's forests, especially in the eastern part of the state.

There are many **food chains** and **food webs** that make up the forest **habitats** of Ohio. A food chain shows how different plants and animals in a habitat rely on one another for food. One species becomes food for another. When food chains are combined, a food web is created.

Ohio Forest Food Web

Each food chain within the food web in each of Ohio's forests begins with the plants. Animals that eat the plants in the forest, such as ants or white-tailed deer, are next on the food chain. A gray catbird or wild turkey may then come along and eat the ants. Then a raccoon might eat the bird, continuing the food chain.

Streams, Lakes, and Rivers

Glaciers of **prehistoric** times created most of Ohio's hills, plains, and valleys. Glaciers also formed many of the state's **streams,** rivers, and lakes. A stream is a flow of water that empties into a river. A river empties into a lake, ocean, or other large body of water. From high in the air, Ohio's streams and rivers look like thousands of veins—some large, others small and narrow—forming a delicate pattern across the state. Ohio's rivers and lakes are linked to each other and to smaller streams, or **tributaries,** that flow into them.

There are more than 60,000 miles of streams in Ohio. That is more miles than you would travel if you went twice around Earth. Most rivers in the state are simply lengthy streams more than 100 miles long.

The Ohio River—Ohio's largest stream—spans 451 miles along the southern border of the state.

The seed pods of the yellow spotted jewelweed burst open when touched.

Ohio has more than 2,000 lakes. The waters of Lake Erie, one of the Great Lakes, cover about 3,500 square miles on Ohio's northern border. The Lake Erie border stretches for 256 miles along northwestern Ohio.

PLANTS

Sycamore, cottonwood, walnut, and elm trees grow along the banks of Ohio's rivers and **streams.** Wildflowers such as bellworts, columbine, and Virginia bluebells dot the banks of these waterways. In late spring, if you smell the scent of licorice, there might be some sweet cicely nearby. The orange or yellow blossomed jewelweed blooms from mid-summer to fall.

ANIMALS

Many bird species live in the trees overlooking Ohio's streams and lakes. Canada geese and great blue heron can be seen near the water's edge. Ohio's biggest bird of **prey,** the bald eagle, makes its home around Lake Erie

The great blue heron is one of the largest birds found in Ohio.

River otters are found in more than 40 counties in Ohio.

and some of Ohio's streams. The eagle finds fish, its favorite food, in these waters. It swoops down to the water's surface and catches the fish with its **talons.** Sometimes the eagle stands along the edges of a stream and uses its beak to catch the fish swimming upstream.

Mammals also make their homes near Ohio's rivers and lakes. River otters are one **species** of mammal. These very social animals are one of the few animals that continue to play even as adults. The otters are **carnivores.** They prey on fish, frogs, rabbits, and other animals in their **habitat.**

The beaver uses the bark and twigs of the trees found near Ohio's streams for food. It builds dams and lodges with the sticks and mud it finds in its habitat. Muskrats, which look much like beavers, are common in Ohio's streams. They can be seen swimming across the waterways, carrying leaves and plants to make their homes.

Amphibians and reptiles all depend on streams for food, for shelter, and as a **breeding** area. Salamanders, frogs, turtles, snakes, and lizards all make use of Ohio's streams and the moist soil found next to the streams. Eight kinds of turtles—including the painted turtle and the snapping turtle—live in Ohio's **streams.** The snapping turtle

Painted turtles live in water most of the time, but they often sun themselves on logs.

Backswimmers have a painful bite, so they are sometimes called water bees.

• •

gets its name because of its powerful jaws. For this reason, it is considered dangerous. The meat of this turtle is the one most often used to make turtle soup.

The northern watersnake is Ohio's largest stream snake. It can grow up to 42 inches long.

Among the 1,200 different kinds of insects in Ohio is the backswimmer. It is found in Ohio's ponds, lakes, and slow-moving streams. This insect got its name because it actually spends most of its time swimming on its back. Its body is shaped a little like a boat. Although backswimmers are only a half-inch long, they sometimes eat tadpoles and small fish.

More than 100 different kinds of dragonflies are found in Ohio. Adult dragonflies are several inches long, and are very bright and colorful. The common green darner dragonfly is found throughout Ohio. In late summer,

• • • • • • • • • • • • • • • • •

Most adult dragonflies only live for a month or two.

A Clean Home for Fish

More than 150 species of fish live in Ohio's streams. Protecting and keeping streams clean ensures that these fish will continue to make their home here.

Largemouth and smallmouth bass, sauger, bluegill, walleye, trout, and catfish are among the fishing favorites. Another favorite sport fish is muskie, either Great Lakes muskie in Lake Erie or Ohio muskie, found in the streams and **tributaries** of the Ohio River. The largest muskie caught in Ohio weighed 55 pounds.

The flathead catfish (above)—found in the Ohio River and many of its tributaries—is even bigger than the muskie. It can grow to more than four feet long and can weigh 80 pounds or more.

swarms of about a million of these insects have been recorded. Most likely they are feeding on other insects or **migrating.**

WATER WILDLIFE

The creek chub is a common fish, found in nearly all of Ohio's streams. Unlike other freshwater fish, it is able to live in somewhat **polluted** conditions. Carp, another common fish, live in warm ponds, lakes, and streams in all 88 counties of Ohio.

Channel catfish is common in Ohio's waters. The Ohio Department of Natural Resources **stocks** this fish. That means it raises this fish in **hatcheries** and then releases it in lakes and rivers. Channel catfish are bluish-silver in color.

Salmon is not a **native** Ohio fish. But coho salmon swim in Lake Erie and spawn in the Huron and Chagrin

Rivers. The coho salmon was first introduced in Ohio in the late 1800s. This fish is native to the Pacific Northwest. It is found in the waters of states like Washington and Oregon. To help keep numbers of salmon high, Ohio **streams** are **stocked** with this fish.

The walleye is one of the most important fish in Lake Erie. It was an important source of food for Ohio's **prehistoric** people, Native Americans, and early European settlers. Today, the walleye is one of the most important game fish in Lake Erie. For this reason, the lake is often called the Walleye Capital of the World. Walleyes are also found in several of Ohio's inland lakes. The fish are released in the lakes after being raised in **hatcheries.**

The walleye has an olive-colored back, white stomach, whitish eyes, and sharp teeth.

Wetlands

When European settlers first arrived in Ohio, they were eager to build towns and cities almost everywhere—except for places where the land was soggy. These places are called **wetlands.** They are covered with shallow water much of the year or have water-logged soil.

One of the state's largest wetlands was once located along Lake Erie in the northwestern corner of the state. The settlers called it the Black **Swamp.** They did not think the area was good for farming. The Black Swamp section of Ohio was very large—about the size of the state of Connecticut. Several other smaller **marshy** areas also dotted the state, but none were as large as the Black Swamp.

The settlers were correct. The Black Swamp was not good for farming. It was not good for supporting buildings.

*Wetland **habitats** support many types of animals and plants.*

Cattails are weeds that grow throughout Ohio's wetlands.

But swamps were and are a perfect **environment** for certain plants, trees, and animals. During **prehistoric** times, Ohio's **wetland** areas were home to many large **mastodons.** The Burning Tree mastodon, named for the golf course on which it was found, was discovered in a wetland region in Licking County, in central Ohio, in 1989. Construction workers discovered the mastodon's bones as they dug in a **marshy** region.

DRAINING THE BLACK SWAMP

Long after prehistoric mammals left, and even after the state was settled, a group of **Mennonite** farm families came to northwestern Ohio. They **immigrated** to the United States from Germany and Switzerland in the 1800s. When they reached Ohio, they thought they could make good farmland out of the Black **Swamp.** They drained the water and developed some of the most **fertile** farmland in Ohio. As a result, the large wetland area disappeared, and so did the plants, trees, and animals that lived there. Today the Black Swamp is known as farmland.

PLANTS OF THE WETLANDS

Today, trees such as oak, maple, and ash are found in Ohio's remaining **wetlands.** Most of the wetlands are located in the northern and western parts of the state.

Plants such as cattails and buttonbush also grow in Ohio's wetlands. Buttonbush, with its rounded white flowers and glossy leaves, starts blooming in the middle of spring.

*The bad odor of the skunk cabbage attracts the insects that **pollinate** it.*

Colorful wildflowers decorate wetland grounds. The exact colors vary, depending upon the season. The smelly skunk cabbage is the first sign of spring in the wetlands of Ohio. It is a **native** plant to Ohio.

Another sign of spring in Ohio's wetlands is the marsh marigold. Its bright yellow flowers cover wet, marshy areas. Later in the spring and summer, pink swamp milkweed and northern blue flag appear. All of these plants are native to Ohio.

ANIMALS OF THE WETLANDS

Many animals prefer living in a wetland to living in a dry **environment.** Reptiles and amphibians **thrive** in wet areas.

The Eastern garter snake is one of Ohio's wetlands reptiles. This snake is the most common of Ohio's garter snakes. The

Marsh marigold grows from shallow water or on ground just above the water.

The spotted salamander spends much of its life underground.

eastern garter snake has a dark body with three stripes. A thin stripe is on its back, and a thicker stripe is on each of its sides. The eastern garter snake feeds on the frogs, toads, salamanders, and mice found in its **wetland habitat.**

One kind of amphibian that lives in Ohio's wetlands is the spotted salamander. It feeds on other amphibians and large insects found in the wetlands. The spotted salamander is a **burrower.**

The numbers of amphibians and reptiles declined when Ohio's wetlands started to disappear. However, they are now growing as small wetland areas increase.

Many other animals, including the jumping mouse, beaver, muskrat, bald eagle, and mink thrive in wetland conditions. Birds such as herons and bluebirds also make their home in Ohio's wetlands.

Sheldon Marsh

Near Cedar Point Amusement Park, located in northern Ohio along Lake Erie, is a path that leads to Sheldon Marsh State Nature Preserve. During the spring, birds flying north stop here to rest and feed. Other birds, especially waterfowl like herons and ducks, live along the lake. The marshes along Lake Erie also attract bald eagles. During the summer, the beautiful cardinal wildflower covers the **swamp** with its bright red color.

PROTECTING THE WETLANDS

Nature preserves and parks in Ohio have wetland areas. Visitors to these places can observe life in this unique **ecosystem.**

Ohioans are working to restore wetlands throughout the state. On public land, the Division of Wildlife continues to work with state **legislators** to make laws that will protect wetlands. It also provides money to **restore** wetlands on private land in the hope that wildlife will live there once again.

Wild mink are small and secretive. They are rarely seen by humans.

Ohio's Bogs

One special kind of wetland found in Ohio is the **bog.** This type of wetland dates back to the last Ice Age. Bogs were formed when ice that was buried in the land melted as the **glaciers** began moving back. Dead plants then began decaying in the bogs. The decayed plant material is called peat. The bogs that exist today are a fraction of the size they once were. Laws now protect these bogs so their ecosystems will not disappear.

Brown's Lake Bog in Wayne County is an example of a bog habitat in Ohio. Very rare plants bloom there. They include the marsh fivefinger and the pitcher plant, shown here. The pitcher plant got its name from its shape. It is a unique plant because it is a **carnivore.** The inside of the plant is lined with hairs that trap insects. A part of the plant contains special juices that help the plant eat the insects.

Prairies

Many **ecosystems** in Ohio, such as the **swamp** and forest, include many trees. But there is an ecosystem in Ohio where few trees grow: the **prairie.** When settlers first arrived in Ohio, there were patches of prairie land. These were located in western Ohio and looked like the prairies found in the western part of the United States. Nearly all of Ohio's prairies have been made into farmland. Today, prairies make up only a very small part of Ohio.

PLANT LIFE ON A PRAIRIE

Many kinds of plants grow on the prairie, but the most common kinds are grasses. Grasses have deep roots and can live where the soil is dry and sandy.

Some of Ohio's prairies, however, are not so dry. These small spots are called wet prairies, and are scattered with oak trees. These are places where the oak trees grow without other trees around. The soil in these places is too dry for most trees, but burr oak is one tree that can survive in the soil of this unique ecosystem.

Many weeds, grasses, and other plants grow in a prairie, while trees are more rare.

26

Tall prairie grasses sometimes grow up to ten feet tall, and they often have flowers. Typical **native** grasses found in Ohio include big blue stem, little blue stem, Indian grass, switch grass, and prairie cordgrass. Black-eyed Susans, purple coneflowers, and blazing star are colorful examples of prairie wildflowers.

Native prairies have mostly been overtaken by nonnative species planted by farmers. Grasses such as timothy grass, orchard grass, and brome grass are grown on farms for hay. These take over the area and prevent native species from growing. Grassland was not common to eastern Ohio in the past, but today, pockets of grasslands bloom in Muskingum, Coshocton, and Jackson Counties.

Prairie cordgrass is another grass that is native to Ohio.

Karner Blue Butterfly

The prairie's Karner blue butterfly is a small butterfly about one inch wide across its wings. The butterfly depends on prairie plants for food. The Karner blue caterpillar depends especially on the wild lupine. The wild lupine is the only plant on which the caterpillar feeds. Today, the Karner blue butterfly is on Ohio's **endangered** species list. It is being **reintroduced** near Toledo.

Ring-necked pheasants live throughout northwestern Ohio.

ANIMAL LIFE

Ohio's **prairies** are also home to many **species** of insects. Moths, butterflies, grasshoppers, and ants are just a few of the insects living in a prairie. Some of these insects, such as the clouded sulfur butterfly, help to **pollinate** the many colorful prairie flowers.

Several species of nesting birds live in Ohio's prairies. The eastern meadowlark feeds on the insects found in the prairie **habitat,** such as crickets and grasshoppers. It also feeds on grains and weed seeds. Like the meadowlark, the ring-necked pheasant feeds on grains such as oats and insects found in the prairies.

Meadow voles feed on grasses and seeds found in prairie habitats.

The northern short-tailed shrew is about the size of an adult rabbit.

Meadow voles are found throughout Ohio's prairies. These animals have short, brown fur, with gray stomachs. Voles are known for the long underground tunnels they **burrow** and for the paths they make through the grass. They feed on the grasses and seeds found in the prairies.

One of the many mammals that **prey** on the insects, mice, and plants of Ohio's prairies is the short-tailed shrew. This type of shrew has poison grooves on its **incisors.** When it bites a mouse, the poison kills the mouse quickly.

Other mammals found on Ohio's prairies include the striped skunk, the 13-lined ground squirrel, and the coyote.

Thirteen-lined ground squirrels eat crickets, grasshoppers, and seeds in Ohio's prairies.

Wildlife in Cities and Towns

In addition to living and growing in the forests, lakes, **streams,** wetlands, and **prairies,** many plants and animals of Ohio today live and grow in the state's towns and cities. These are called **urban** areas.

Urban areas have replaced many forest **habitats** of plants and animals in Ohio. Plants and animals have **adapted** to survive in urban areas where people live and work. Animals other than pets that have adapted to life in these areas are known as urban wildlife. These wild animals include the animals that live in Ohio's cities and **suburban** areas. They are able to live there because people have created habitats in which these animals can survive.

ANIMALS IN THE CITY

Many mammals make their homes in Ohio's cities. Gray squirrels live in the large trees in neighborhoods and parks. The opossum and raccoon are often seen searching for food around neighborhood garbage cans.

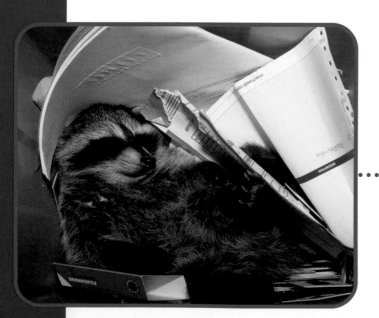

Paper in a garbage bin makes a safe bed for an urban raccoon.

The woodchuck is known for the tunnels it builds in the yards and gardens of Ohio's cities. The woodchucks travel in and out of the tunnels. They build more than one entrance to help them escape from **predators.**

The house mouse is found throughout cities and towns in Ohio. It eats the human food and garbage found there.

Although the red fox may prefer to make Ohio's forests its home, it also makes its home in some of Ohio's suburbs. The brown bat uses some of Ohio's city buildings and bridges as summer **roosting** sites. The eastern cottontail rabbit makes its home in the shrubs and plants of city yards and gardens.

Coyotes have also been seen in Ohio's urban areas. They often use abandoned buildings for their homes. They find their food in garbage cans.

Urban animals find food and shelter in large trees, just as they would in their natural habitat.

Many kinds of birds are found in Ohio's cities and towns. They include the blue jay, American robin, mourning dove, and cardinal.

Other animals include reptiles such as the eastern garter snake and insects such as butterflies. Monarch butterflies are found throughout Ohio. The tiger swallowtail butterfly lives in parks and **suburbs** of Ohio. It is beneficial to Ohioans because it helps to **pollinate** the flowers in the neighborhood gardens.

Peregrine Falcon

An interesting **urban** animal is the peregrine falcon. In the wild, peregrine falcons like to nest in stone cliffs. But these birds have creatively **adapted** to city conditions. They use the stone skyscrapers in Ohio's larger cities, which are a bit like stone cliffs to these birds. Twelve pairs have nested on top of tall buildings around Ohio. Most of the falcons have been named. Bandit and Katie lived downtown in Columbus until Katie's death. Another falcon named Bandit and his mate Chesapeake live in Akron. Flash and Liberty live in Cleveland. Other peregrine falcons live in Cincinnati, Toledo, and Dayton.

The peregrine falcon is on Ohio's **endangered** species list. Peregrine falcons became endangered in the 1960s after they were exposed to the harmful DDT **pesticide** used by humans. The pesticide prevented females from producing healthy eggs. Their population soon decreased. A government program to raise young falcons and reintroduce them to the wild has increased the population.

Boxelder trees usually grow to be less than 50 feet high.

PLANTS IN THE CITY

The boxelder is a tree that is found throughout all of Ohio. The name of the tree comes from the fact that in the past the wood from the tree had been used to make wooden crates and boxes.

Buckeye trees, Ohio's state tree, are found in parks and neighborhoods in every county. The leaves have five leaflets. Thick, prickly shells cover the shiny brown nuts, or buckeyes. Buckeye trees are usually about 30 to 50 feet tall, but the record height is 82 feet. The record is held by State Champion Big Tree, grown in North Bend, west of Cincinnati.

Other trees found in Ohio's urban areas include the white ash and the red maple. Wildflowers such as the wild violet grow in many of Ohio's cities and suburbs.

Buckeye seeds are shiny dark brown, with a light-colored spot that gives them the appearance of a deer's eye.

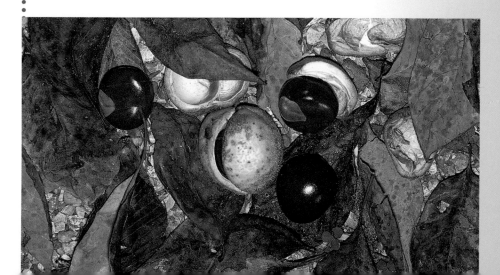

How to Plant a Buckeye Tree

The Ohio Division of Forestry provides instructions on how to plant a buckeye tree. Planting buckeye trees from seeds is easy. Once the seeds germinate, or sprout, the seeds grow quickly. In less than ten years, there will be buckeyes on the tree.

1. Gather buckeyes in the fall. Collect twice as many as you think you will need, because it is likely that only about half will grow. 2. Plant the buckeyes in a shady spot as soon as possible. Do not let them dry out. 3. Break up the soil and plant them about three inches deep. 4. Scatter the holes about, and put only one buckeye seed in each hole. 5. Then add about three inches of mulch. 6. You can also put straw on top to protect the seeds during the winter, but remove the straw and mulch the following spring. 7. In the spring, be sure to water the seeds each week. 8. After the seeds germinate, water and fertilize them until early fall. Do not overwater the seeds.

Squirrels will try to dig up the seeds. Place a piece of chicken wire over the seeds before adding the mulch layer if there are squirrels near where you are planting. Remember to remove the screen when you clear off the mulch. After a year, you can dig up the seedlings and replant them where you want your buckeye trees to grow.

Endangered Species

Ohio's forests, **wetlands,** and **prairies** almost disappeared completely after European settlers arrived in the 1700s and turned these natural areas into farmland, factories, homes, cities, and roads. As more settlers arrived, transportation increased, cities grew, and even more people moved to Ohio.

What effect did this have on the wildlife **habitats** in these **ecosystems?** What happened to all the plants and animals that once called Ohio home? In many cases, they disappeared when their habitat or living conditions changed or disappeared. As a result, some of Ohio's wildlife has become **endangered** or **extinct.**

The bobcat is a *native* species of Ohio. It is now endangered in the state.

Ohio's Endangered Wildlife

There are a number of plants and animals on Ohio's endangered species list. A few of these species are listed here:

Mammals:

Allegheny woodrat

bobcat

black bear

Indiana myotis

Reptiles:

copperbelly water snake

eastern plains garter snake

timber rattlesnake

eastern massasauga

Plants:

lakeside daisy

running buffalo clover (pictured below)

northern wild monkshood

eastern prairie fringed orchid

Amphibians:

blue-spotted salamander

green salamander

cave salamander

Fish:

Ohio lamprey

pugnose minnow

popeye shiner

speckled chub

Insects:

Hine's emerald dragonfly

frosted elfin butterfly

unexpected cycnia moth

Ohio cave beetle

REASONS WILDLIFE IS ENDANGERED

One of the main reasons that some plants and animals in Ohio have become **endangered** is the loss of **habitats.** As habitats such as forests and **wetlands** have been cleared for farming and building, animals that live there, such as the river otter and the osprey have become endangered.

Yet another reason for wildlife loss is **pollution.** Pollution hurts both humans and wildlife. It damages plant and animal habitats. Farming and factory waste poison

Ohio Wildlife Refuges

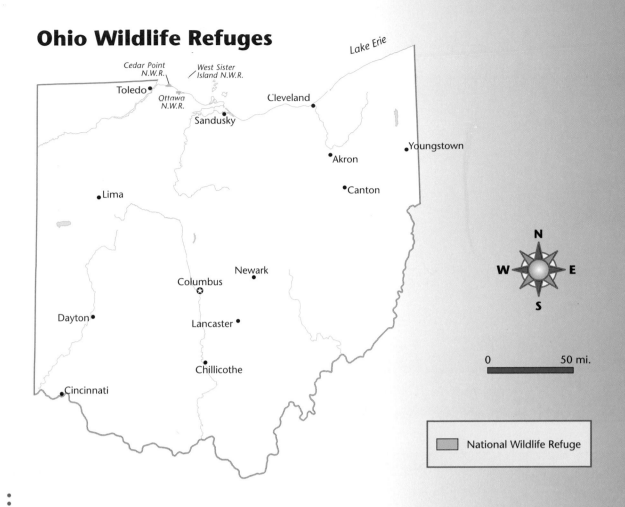

National Wildlife Refuges were set aside to help protect Ohio's native species.

rivers and lakes. The pollution of Ohio's waterways has caused several types of fish to become endangered.

There were no hunting, trapping, or fishing laws to protect wildlife when people first lived in Ohio. Wildlife populations decreased when animals such as the elk and the white-tailed deer were overhunted.

BLACK BEAR

Black bears are the most common bear **species** in the United States. There are only a few black bears in Ohio. They were overhunted and lost their homes when the forests were cleared. In the 1850s, the bears moved to other, more densely wooded areas. Today, the black bear

*As **omnivores,** bears eat plants—usually berries, herbs, nuts—and dead animals. They are called black bears, but they can also be brown. Adults can weigh up to 300 pounds.*

is a protected species. This means that it cannot be hunted or trapped. About 50 black bears have been seen in recent years in the eastern parts of Ohio.

TIMBER RATTLESNAKE

The timber rattlesnake is the most dangerous snake in the northeastern United States. It is usually found in the wooded, hilly countryside in southern Ohio. This poisonous snake eats squirrels, mice, and small birds. Timber rattlesnakes cannot live in **urban** areas. They have become endangered because so many of Ohio's forests, which are the the snakes' natural **habitat,** have been destroyed.

BARN OWL

The barn owl lives in Ohio's grassy fields and **wetlands.** These owls arrived in southwestern Ohio in the mid-1800s, after much of Ohio's forests were turned into farmland. By the 1930s, barn owls were found in 84 of Ohio's counties. Then in the 1940s, as the number of farms began to decrease, the barn owls' habitats also began to decrease. By the 1970s, only a small number of

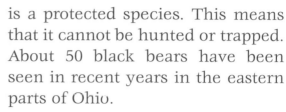

The timber rattlesnake will rise up and shake its rattle before striking.

barn owls lived in some parts of Ohio. Today, the barn owl is an **endangered** species. **Conservation** programs are working to increase the number of these animals.

NORTHERN WILD MONKSHOOD

A **threatened** plant species in Ohio is the northern wild monkshood. Northern wild monkshood has only been found in Ohio, Iowa, Wisconsin, and New York.

The monkshood's habitat is being threatened for several reasons. In some places livestock have grazed and trampled it. People have walked through the monkshood's habitat.

Logging, the building of highways, and the uses of pesticides have all contributed to the monkshood's decline.

LAKESIDE DAISY

There are more than 200 types of endangered plants in Ohio. The rare lakeside daisy is one of these plants. It is named for Lakeside, Ohio, which is located near the daisy's best-known sites. It is illegal to pick or destroy this flower. This rare plant lives in only three states—Ohio, Michigan, and Illinois. Ohio has the largest population, although it is very small.

The lakeside daisy grows along Lake Erie on the Marblehead Peninsula in Ohio. It lives in a unique **habitat** called a limestone grassland. This spot is the lakeside daisy's only natural habitat in the state. The daisy has become **endangered** partly because people destroy its habitat while mining the surrounding limestone.

SUCCESS STORIES

The **marshy** shores of Lake Erie offer a healthy habitat for more than 30 types of endangered animals. One of them, the bald eagle, is showing up in record numbers. Each winter, wildlife officials count all the bald eagles in the state. The eagles seem to prefer the shores of Lake Erie, but they recently have been counted in 44 of Ohio's 88 counties. When the program to help bald eagles began in Ohio in 1979, there were only six in the entire state. Today, there are more than 250.

Another success story is the river otter, which had almost disappeared from its habitat around Ohio's rivers and **streams.** Work to protect and **reintroduce** the river otter in northern Ohio was so successful that in 2002, this animal was taken off Ohio's endangered species list.

The bald eagle, a symbol for the United States, has a life expectancy of fifteen to twenty years.

Extinct Species

When many people think of **extinct** animals, they think of dinosaurs. But Ohio's **fossil** record shows no evidence of dinosaurs at all. This does not mean that dinosaurs never lived here. Most scientists think it is very likely that dinosaurs once roamed Ohio's lands during the Mesozoic Era, which lasted from about 245 million years ago to about 66 million years ago. However, there are no rocks left in Ohio from that time period. Without rocks, scientists cannot find fossils.

Scientists have, however, found fossils of other ancient, extinct **species** from other time periods in Ohio. For example, during the Paleozoic Era, which lasted from 570 million years ago to 260 million years ago, Ohio was covered by a tropical ocean. For this reason, scientists have found the fossils of a wide variety of extinct sea creatures in Ohio.

Around 360 million years ago, during the Paleozoic Era, a fish called *Dunkleosteus terrelli*—meaning "terrible fish"—swam in the waters around what is now Cleveland. This fish had huge jaws, and its giant head—which could be ten feet long—was covered with armor. Growing to a total length of 15 to 30 feet, this fish was most likely a feared **predator.**

This reconstructed skull of a Dunkleosteus terrelli *is in the Cleveland Museum of Natural History.*

*Brachiopods were a type of invertebrate. That means they had no backbone. They lived on the sea floor, **burrowing** in the mud. Brachiopods ate by opening their shells and filtering food from the water.*

Fossils of clam-like animals known as brachiopods have been found in Ohio. These animals lived in the water that covered Ohio in the Ordovician Period, a time between 500 and 438 million years ago.

More than 100 years ago, the Conway **mastodon** was discovered in Clarke County in Ohio. It is similar to the Burning Tree Mastodon. Both mastodons stood about ten feet tall at the shoulders.

In 1919, workers digging land for the Huffman Dam near Dayton, Ohio, discovered the fossil of a trilobite. The Huffman Dam trilobite was the biggest trilobite ever found in one piece. This water creature lived in what is now southwestern Ohio about 440 million years ago. Today, the trilobite is Ohio's state fossil.

The Huffman Dam trilobite, found near Dayton, is about 14.5 inches long.

The ivory-billed woodpecker once made Ohio its home. The **remains** of this bird have been found in places in Ross, Scioto, and Muskingum counties. Scientists believe that it lived in Ohio between 1300 and 1700 C.E. No one knows for sure when the ivory-billed woodpecker actually died out.

The blue pike is another example of an extinct species in Ohio. However, the blue pike became extinct only recently. Large numbers of blue pike once lived in Lake Erie. They were important to Ohio's fishing industry. In the 1950s, about three million blue pike were caught. This overfishing and **pollution** of the waters caused the blue pike to become extinct.

The Carolina parakeet is another extinct animal in Ohio. The last sighting of this bird in Ohio was in 1862. By then, the birds' habitat was replaced by corn fields. Farmers killed the Carolina parakeets because they ruined their crops. Hunters killed them for their colorful feathers. The feathers were used in women's hats.

Passenger pigeons once flew through Ohio by the billions. By the year 1900, however, the last wild passenger pigeon was shot in Pike County, Ohio. The last passenger pigeon in captivity, a bird named

Carolina parakeet

Scientists say that at one time the passenger pigeon outnumbered all other bird species in North America combined.

Martha, died in 1914 at the Cincinnati Zoo. The extinction of the birds was primarily caused by overhunting. Hunters shot the birds for food and for sport. Other causes of the bird's extinction were the destruction of its forest habitat and the fact that it only laid one egg at a time.

THE FUTURE OF OHIO'S WILDLIFE

Some animals moved out of Ohio when their **habitat** was destroyed. They became **extirpated** from the state. Unfortunately, it has not been possible to recover all of the extirpated **species.** Ohio has, however, had success with some species, such as the white-tailed deer.

State and federal laws now protect endangered species and their habitats. The government keeps a list of endangered and **threatened** wildlife. They revise the list at least every five years—sometimes sooner, if necessary.

With continued efforts to protect **endangered** species, Ohio may one day catch a glimpse of what the first settlers saw when they arrived in the state. It may be impossible to fully restore the habitats that once existed, but they certainly can exist on a smaller scale.

Map of Ohio

Ohio

Glossary

adapt   to change in a way that allows an animal or plant to live in new conditions

bill   proposed law to be considered for approval by lawmakers

bog   area of soft, wet soil

breed   to produce offspring

brush   heavy growth of bushes and small trees

burrow   to dig a hole in the ground

carnivore   animal that eats other animals in order to live

coniferous   having cones

conservation   effort to preserve natural resources such as soil, water, and forest from pollution and destruction

culture   ideas, skills, arts, and way of life of a certain people at a certain time

deciduous   losing leaves each year

ecosystem   community of living things, together with the environment in which they live

endangered   at risk or in danger

environment   all the things that surround and affect a person, animal, or plant

extinct   no longer living

extirpated   no longer living in a certain place, having moved to another

fertile   rich, productive

food chain   diagram of the plants and animals that need each other for food within a particular habitat

food web   several food chains combined

fossil   remains or traces of a living thing of long ago

glacier   large sheet of ice that spreads very slowly over land

habitat   natural home of a plant or animal

hatchery   place where fish eggs are hatched

immigrate   to come into a foreign country or region to live

incisors   sharp teeth

legislature   governmental body that makes and changes laws. A member of that body is a legislator.

marsh   wet, low-lying area, often thick with tall grasses

mastodon   large, extinct animal, similar to an elephant, with tusks and shaggy hair. Mastodons usually lived in forests.

Mennonite   group of people whose religion is called Anabaptist, which means "to be baptized again;" group of people who left their homes in Switzerland and Germany in search of religious freedom

migrate   move from one place to another on a regular schedule

native   originally from an area

nursery   place where trees and plants are grown and sold

omnivore animal that eats both plants and animals

pesticide substance used to destroy pests, such as DDT

pollinate process by which plants reproduce

pollution state of being impure or dirty

prairie large area of grassland

predator animal that eats another animal

prehistoric from the time before history was written

prey animal hunted for food by another animal

reintroduce bring in again

remains what is left behind; a dead body

resource valuable thing that can be made useful. There are natural and humanmade resources.

roost place on which birds pirch

seedling young plant that is grown from seed

species group of living things that resemble one another, have common ancestors, and can breed with one another

stock supply

stream flow of water that empties into a river

suburb city or town just outside a large city. Suburban means having to do with a suburb.

swamp wet, low-lying area with trees growing in a shallow water

talon claw of a bird

threatened facing possible coming danger

thrive do well

tributary stream that flows into another stream or other body of water

urban having to do with cities

wetland very wet, low-lying land

More Books to Read

Brown, Dottie. *Ohio.* Minneapolis: Lerner Publishing Group, 1995.

Davis, Jeffrey G. and Scott A. Menze. *Atlas of Ohio's Frogs and Toads.* Columbus, OH: Ohio Biological Survey, 2000.

Fradin, Dennis Brindell. *Ohio.* Danbury, Conn.: Scholastic Library, 2000.

Sherrow, Victoria. *Ohio.* Tarrytown, NY: Marshall Cavendish, 1998.

Thompson, Kathleen. *Ohio.* Chicago: Raintree, 1996.

Index

About the Author

Marcia Schonberg is a lifelong resident of Ohio. She writes regularly for daily newspapers and regional and national magazines. Her list of books includes the children's book *B is for Buckeye*. A graduate of Ohio State University, Schonberg now makes her home in Lexington with her husband Bill.